A Fine Line Between . . .

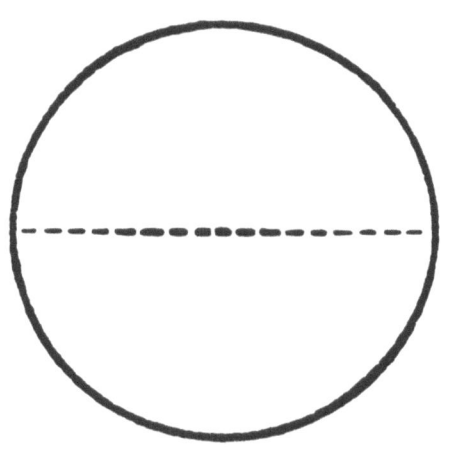

Prof. ODDFELLOW's Forgotten Wisdom

Abstraction

Obfuscation

$$\frac{Absurdity}{Profundity}$$

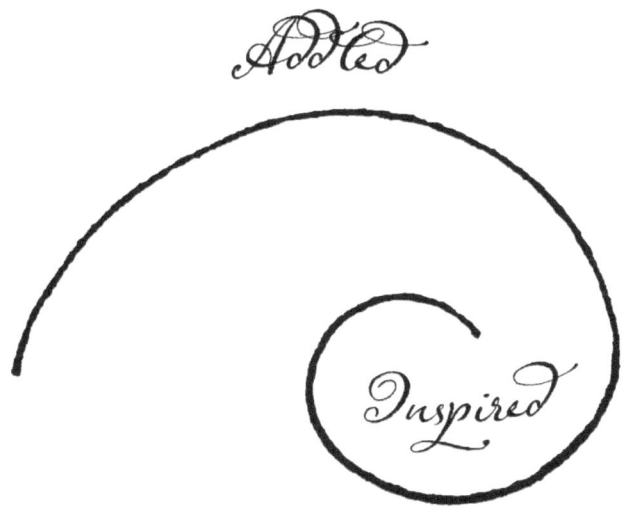

Addled

Inspired

Agony

Ecstasy

Alchemy

Chemistry

$$\frac{\textit{Ambition}}{\textit{Greed}}$$

Analysis

Opinion

Angst

Anger

Anonymity

Celebrity

Art

———————————————

Crime

Assertion

Aggression

Audacity

Atrocity

Audibility

Annoyance

Bargaining

Niggling

Beachfront Property

Crashing Surf

Bitter

---------→

Hopeful

Bold Moves

Dysfunctional Maneuvers

Brilliance

Madness

Brilliantly Good

Thrillingly Awful

Casual

Careless

Ceremony

Spoof

Champion

Runner-up

Chaos

Order

Character

Caricature

Cheap

Sleazy

Civilization

Savagery

Coincidence

———————————→

Fate

Comedy

Suspense

Comic

Tragic

Commerce

—————————

Banking

Commitment

Entrapment

$$\frac{Confidence}{Cockiness}$$

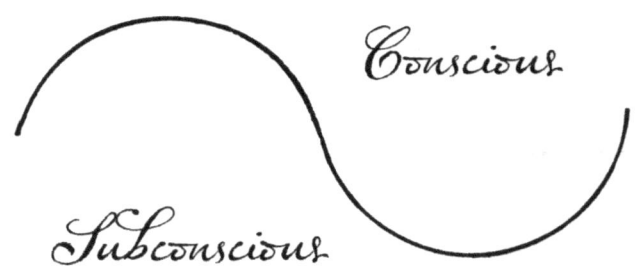

Consensus Building

Collusion

Conservatives

Reformers

Containment

Imprisonment

Control

Oblivion

$$\frac{Cops}{Criminals}$$

Courage

Rashness

"Cult"

Crap

Danger

Safety

Detachment

Desire

Dignity

————————————————

Farce

Dilettantism

———————————————————

Connoisseurship

Diplomacy

Cowardice

$$\frac{Discipline}{Abuse}$$

Disgraceful Servility

Perilous Insult

Distinction

Separation

Divine

———————————————

Human

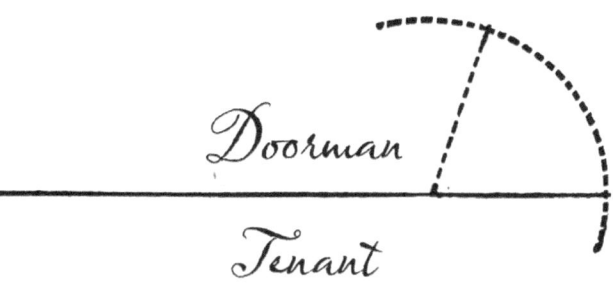

$$\frac{Dreams}{Wakefulness}$$

Dull

Subtle

Education

Entertainment

Embarrassment

Tenderness

Emphasizing Strengths

Outright Bragging

Enough

Too Much

Enthusiasm

Competence

Enthusiasm

Excessiveness

Erotic

Art

Pornography

Excessive Generalization

Over-specification

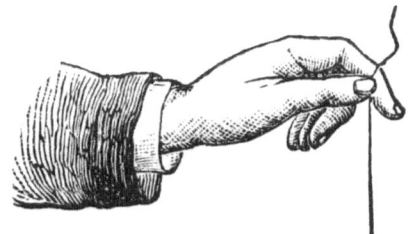

Esoteric   Obscure

Exaltation of the
Conquistador

Despair of
the Shipwrecked

Expounding

Expousing

Exuberance

Disillusionment

Faith

Foolishness

$$\frac{Familiarity}{Strangeness}$$

Fan

———————————————————

Stalker

Feeling Protected

Feeling Controlled

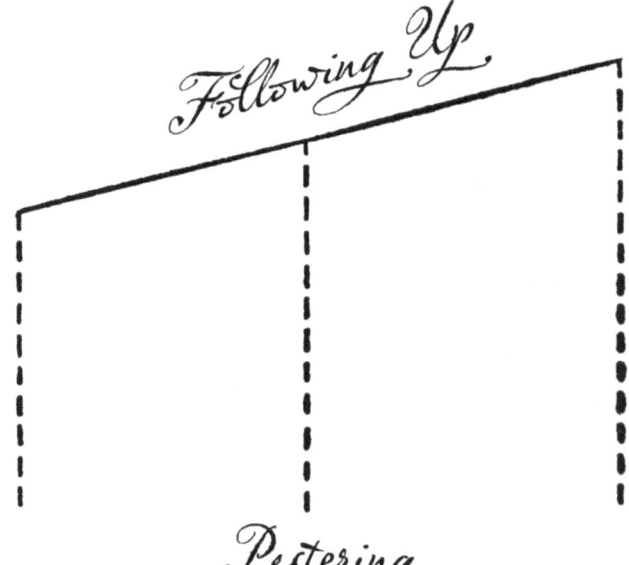

Frankness

Brutality

Gaudy

Imaginative

Generosity

Aggressiveness

Goth

———————————————

Emo

Grassland

Desert

Groove

Rut

Handhold

Foothold

Heaven

Hell

History

Fiction

$$\frac{\text{Hobby}}{\text{Insanity}}$$

Homage

Parody

Horseplay

———————————————————

Conflict

Hospitality

Undue Familiarity

$$\frac{\text{Human Beings}}{\text{Beasts}}$$

Illegal
Dumping

Legally Negotiated
Business Transactions

Imposition

Consent

Innocence

Sexiness

Innocent Fellowship

Emotional Adultery

Interference

Inattention

Irony

Fadedness

$$\frac{Kindness}{Permissiveness}$$

Kitsch

Trash

Laughter

Tears

Living

Dying

Love

Nausea

Lying

_____

Not Telling

Maritime Commerce

Piracy

Marketing

Prostitution

Mastery

Slavery

Nightmare

- - - - - - - - - - - - - - - - - -

Reality

$$\frac{Normality}{Neuroticism}$$

Objectivity

Advocacy

Obsequiousness

Hypocrisy

Obsessive Love

Psychosis

Offering Feedback

Doing the Work

Opera

Broadway

Ordinary

Monstrous

Organized Religion

Organized Crime

Pain Management

Opioid Addiction

Passion

Paranoia

Persistence

←————————————————————————

Pestering

Persuasion

————————————

Propaganda

Persuasion

Coercion

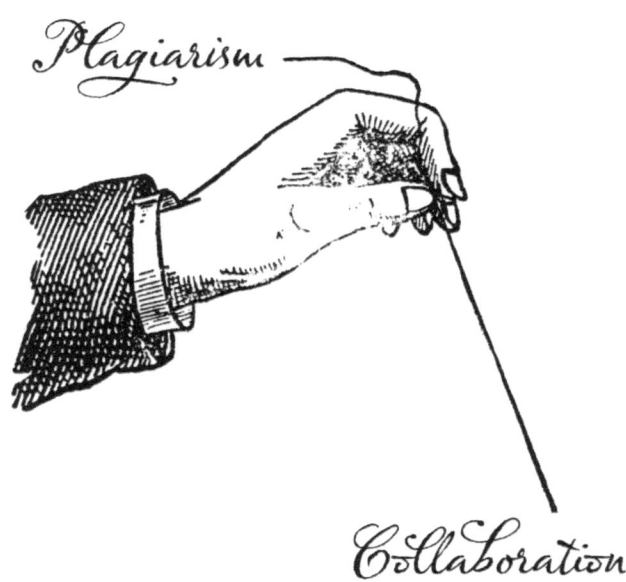

Plagiarism

Collaboration

$$\frac{Pleasure}{Pain}$$

Political Crisis

Media Sensation

Political Success

Historical Infamy

Pressuring

- - - - - - - - - - - - - - - - - - -

Encouaging

Pride

Piousness

Prima Donna

— — — — — — — — — — —

Unemployed Flake

Prose

———————————————

Poetry

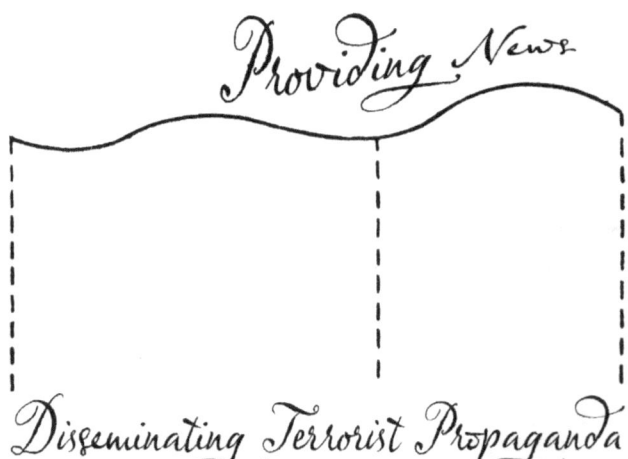

Providing News

Disseminating Terrorist Propaganda

Punk

Poser

Rage

Sorrow

Rape

Seduction

Religion

Politics

Repentance

Masochism

Representation

Reality

Repulsion

Awe

Rhetoric

Poetic

Ruthless

Evil

Sacred

Profane

Saturday Night

Sunday Morning

Science

Showmanship

Saint
Sebastian

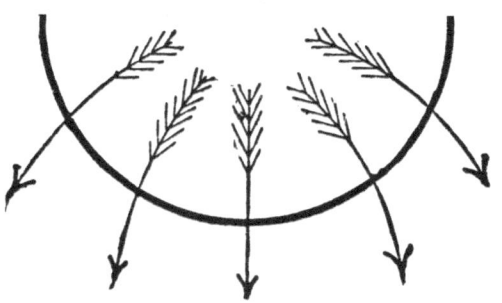

The Cult of Mithras

Sedation

Euthanasia

Self-Love

Selfishness

Sensuality

———————————————

Spirituality

Separate

Separable

Serving Others

Being Eaten Alive

Sexual Admiration

Sexual Harassment

Sincerity

Satire

Smug

Insane

Soldiers

Civilians

Spices

Herbs

Spin

Reality

Spontaneity

————— · ——— · ——— · —— · ——— · ——— ·

Memorization

Standing Relaxed

Posing

Sticking to
the Rock

Yielding
to Gravity

Stupid

Clever

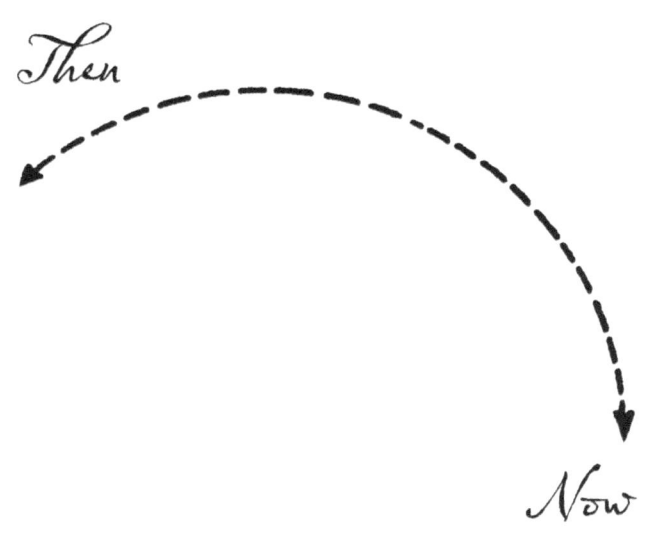

Then

Now

$$Theory$$

___

$$Fantasy$$

This

Anarchy

Tip

Bribe

Titillation

———————————

Provocation

Tradition

Obselescence

Traditional Religion

Forbidden Magic

Tragedy

Bathos

Translation

_____

Composition

Truth

Fiction

Union

———————————————————

Unity

Vanity

Pride

Victim

Rescuer

Well-being

Poverty

Whimsical

———————————————————

Inappropriate

Yourself

Your Subordinates

Zero